I like to play

Bobbie Kalman

 Crabtree Publishing Company

www.crabtreebooks.com

Created by Bobbie Kalman

Author and Editor-in-Chief
Bobbie Kalman

Educational consultants
Elaine Hurst
Joan King
Jennifer King

Notes for adults
Jennifer King

Editors
Kathy Middleton
Crystal Sikkens

Design
Bobbie Kalman
Katherine Berti

Print and production coordinator
Katherine Berti

Prepress technician
Katherine Berti

Photo research
Bobbie Kalman

Photographs by Shutterstock

Library and Archives Canada Cataloguing in Publication

Kalman, Bobbie, 1947-
    I like to play / Bobbie Kalman.

(My world)
Issued also in electronic format.
ISBN 978-0-7787-9549-0 (bound).--ISBN 978-0-7787-9574-2 (pbk.)

    1. Ball games--Juvenile literature. I. Title. II. Series: My world
(St. Catharines, Ont.)

GV861.K34 2011   j796.3   C2010-907311-8

Library of Congress Cataloging-in-Publication Data

Kalman, Bobbie.
    I like to play / Bobbie Kalman.
       p. cm. -- (My world)
    ISBN 978-0-7787-9574-2 (pbk. : alk. paper) -- ISBN 978-0-7787-9549-0
(reinforced library binding : alk. paper) -- ISBN 978-1-4271-9656-9
(electronic (pdf))
    1. Ball games--Juvenile literature. I. Title. II. Series.

GV861.K35 2011
796.3--dc22
                                                2010046418

Crabtree Publishing Company
www.crabtreebooks.com   1-800-387-7650

Printed in China/022011/RG20101116

Published in Canada
Crabtree Publishing
616 Welland Ave.
St. Catharines, Ontario
L2M 5V6

Published in the United States
Crabtree Publishing
PMB 59051
350 Fifth Avenue, 59th Floor
New York, New York 10118

Published in the United Kingdom
Crabtree Publishing
Maritime House
Basin Road North, Hove
BN41 1WR

Published in Australia
Crabtree Publishing
386 Mt. Alexander Rd.
Ascot Vale (Melbourne)
VIC 3032

Words to know

baseball

basketball

beach ball

golf

jumping ball

soccer

3

I like to play soccer.

I can kick the ball.

I like to play baseball.

I can catch the ball.

I like to play golf.

I can hit the ball.

I like to play basketball.

I can shoot the ball.

I like to play with a beach ball.

I like to play with a jumping ball.

Which ball is a jumping ball?
Which ball is a soccer ball?
Which ball is a beach ball?
Which ball is a basketball?
Which ball is a golf ball?
Which ball is a baseball?

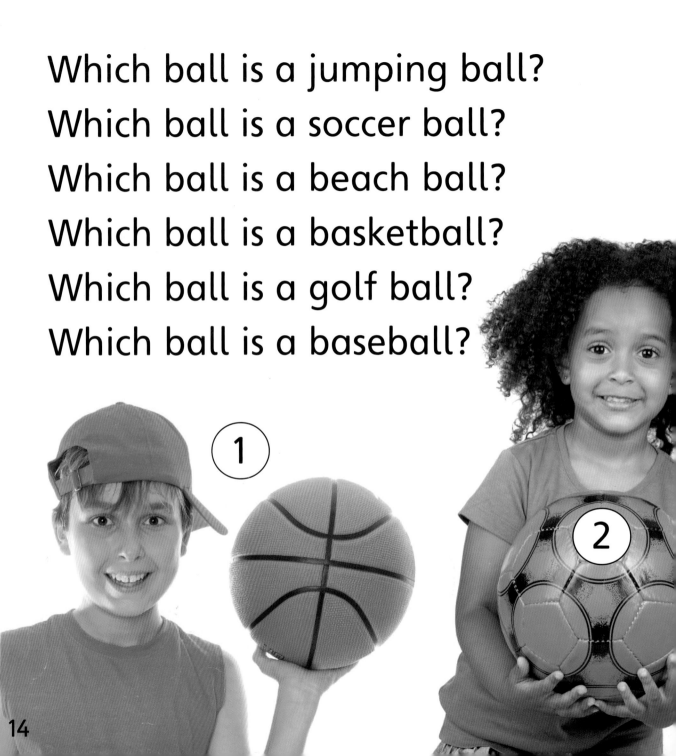

③

④

⑤

⑥

Answers

1. basketball
2. soccer ball
3. baseball
4. jumping ball
5. golf ball
6. beach ball

Notes for adults

Objectives
- to have children identify which sports are played with balls
- to have children identify the types of balls they play with
- to engage children in a discussion about sports and activities they like
- to identify other ways they play

Before reading the book
Write these frequently used words on the board:
a, ball, can, I, is, like, play, the, to, which, with
Ask the children to describe activities they enjoy doing.
"What sports do you like to play? Why?"
"What other activities do you like to do? Why?"
Have the children share experiences about their favorite activities.

Questions after reading the book
Go back through the book and ask the children if they like the activities mentioned. Have them come up with their own reasons why they like each activity.
Ask: "Do you like to play soccer?"

Child: "Yes, I do because I can…"
Bring in the different types of balls from the story. Have the children identify the balls and the sports in which they are used.
Have the children share other words ending in "ball." Examples of other balls: volleyball, dodgeball, tennis ball, and football.

Activity: Make a mural!
Stretch out a long sheet of paper on the floor or wall. Write the phrase "We like to play" in the middle. Have the children draw or paint either their favorite types of ball games or other games they like to play.
Draw large pictures of different balls around the room. Have the children sign their names on the balls they like and write "I like to play…"
Play a listening game. Say: "I like baseball…(or another ball game)." When the children hear your clue, they walk over to the correct ball.

Extension
Bring in pictures of people dressed in the uniforms of particular sports. Have the children guess which sports they play based on their uniforms.

Invite family members to share what they like to play or which activities they like to do. Ask them to bring pictures or short videos of the activities.

For teacher's guide, go to www.crabtreebooks.com/teachersguides